Wisdom to Youth

Freya Blyth

BookLeaf Publishing

WISDOM TO YOUTH
FREYA BLYTH
20
21

From Wisdom to Youth

Ancient Wisdom For Modern Times

© 2021 Freya Blyth

Presentation by *BookLeaf Publishing*

Web: www.bookleafpub.com

E-mail: info@bookleafpub.com

ISBN: 9789358360929

First edition 2021

by

freya tólmi blyth

Freya Blyth lives by the sea in a cosy storybook town in Wales. She enjoys far too many cups of hot chocolate and reading regency based books, while spotting dolphins, to which she always squeals with enthusiasm. She likes slow walkers and fast talkers, and all forms of loving prayer.

Freya studied as an Actor in London, worked in libraries around the world and is currently studying a Creative Writing MA.

ACKNOWLEDGEMENT

Thank you to my spirit sisters, who see my wings
and fly with me.

Thank you to my blyth siblings who brought me joy
from the moment they came into this world.

Thank you finally to my mum, who taught me how
to love Austen, question smooth-talkers and to
always live somewhere that could be from a
children's book. She taught me to laugh and cry and
be a woman.

For the Librarians,
Guardian of Books, Keeper of Stories, Legend
Seekers of Worlds.

"To the girl
who reads by flashlight
who sees dragons in the clouds
who feels most alive in worlds that never were
who knows magic is real
who dreams

This is for you"

- Meagan Spooner, Hunted

This collection of poems is about how the mountains
of my youth have saved me from the valleys of
growing up.

This is the wisdom I wish I had in my youth.
The hand reaching out telling me it is ok, someone
else feels the same. You are not alone, dear reader.

I hope my words comfort you in knowing even
when it's a painful, overwhelming -curl up- or
scream out- kind of day; you were never alone.

This thing called life is a confusing, wonderful mess
and creative explosion of madness.
Please enjoy it, and don't leave litter.

Once Upon a Time

once upon a time
a girl sat lonely
caught in a field
of possibilities
between what will come
what could have been
and what was not chosen.

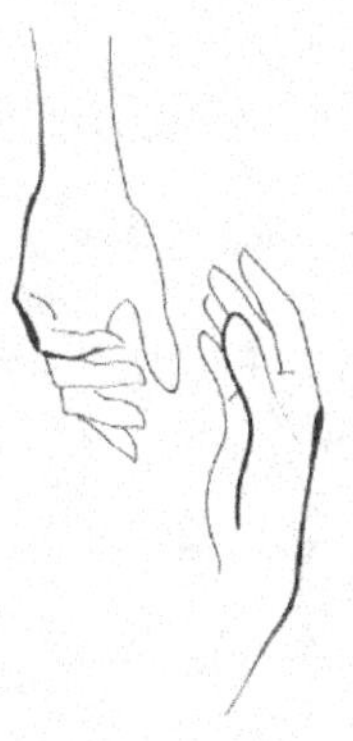

Survivor

How have I lived so long
Survived this mess of a broken world?

With joy and hope tattooed on my forehead
And stamped on my heart.

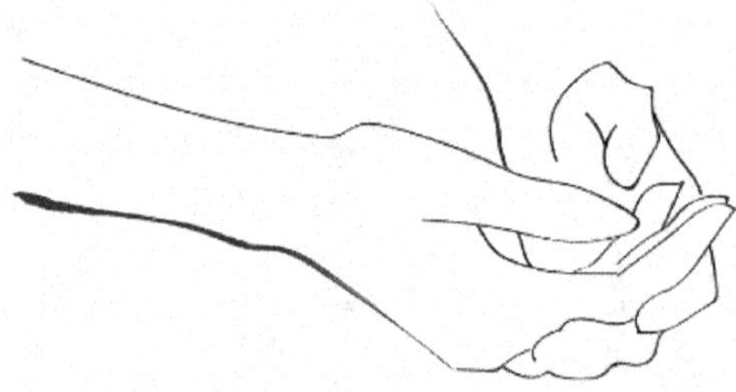

Saviour

Stories taught me that the saviour
Is strong of spirit
Pure of heart
With a Noble character

The princess is beautiful
Patient
Kind and has courage
She is willing to sing through trials
Dance over shards of glass of unkindness
Dream boldly of a different life

She believes in magic
To help or miracles to get her there

They have drawn me a map
Now I know what I must become.
Be a curse breaker
Dancing through trials
Have faith in those around me
Conviction to follow my heart
To be strong, pure, noble
My own Princess Saviour.

Fairytales we tell

When will we learn that princes are not good men
That the princess could spend the time waiting
To learn and grow and break their own chains

At the very least fairytales teach us
Curses can always be broken

Role models

My mum never let me have barbie dolls
Until I, impassioned aged 9, put on a presentation
For why my body image would not be influenced

Little did she know
It was her strength
I would measure myself against

Always 3 inches off

Wisdom is hard-earned
No one promised this was easy
This rolling upward
Struggle we call life

Still, there are valleys of immense beauty
Places to lie down and rest
Beside still waters
Find peace

From Wisdom to Youth

Apply your heart to wisdom
For from your heart comes the wellspring of life.

Guard your heart
Wisdom will become your shield

Youth holds naive, beautiful joy.
A freedom to experience
The world through

Let joy be your sword.

Field of Gold

I know a meadow
far beyond
What you think is right
Or I think is wrong
Will you meet me there?

Rumi showed me the way
My soul collapsed there
In relief and gratitude
Found a home amidst the flowers
As I gave up
Trying to speak
About fragments of the world
Instead, I filled with birdsong

Wings

Hope and sorrow are sisters
Birds in the same flight
Migrating with the months
They cross
Returning to warmer climates

Sweetheart

Do not call out
Hey Sweetheart
expecting me to answer,
I gave up that name
a long time ago.

Ghosting

When you vanish
Like mist in the morning sun,
As though the heat was too strong for you-
Even in its first rays,
It means I have to hide my light
Or lose you

That I'm 'too much'
Even at my beginning

You stop responding
Which cuts me
As though my arm is missing
Feeling for a bag I left at home
The phantom missing boyfriend
I want you to be here so much
I'll pay anything
From myself
I become in debt to my soul
One day I have to settle the accounts
A reckoning with me, soul and spirit.
For all that I lost and gave away.
you are never too much.

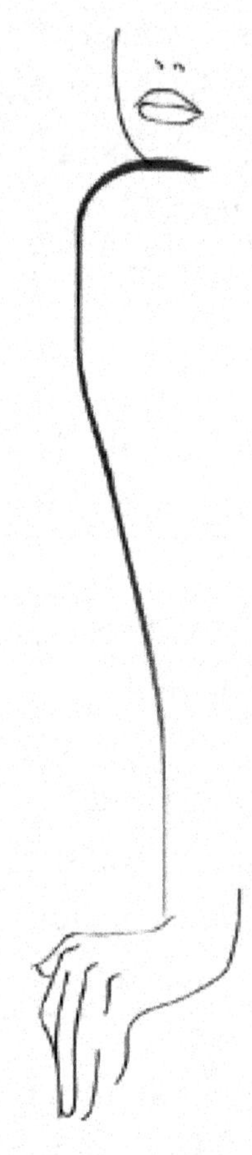

Scream

Sometimes my voice wants to scream so loud,
I have to suffocate myself, face in a pillow,
To keep from shaking the walls, with my cries.

The Cost of Kindness

What did kindness cost you?
Noting, it was a free gift
Within you from birth.

Control

The claws reach for me
I scream
But don't move
I want the safety
Of their solid grip

Piercing through my skin
At least I know
Where I am
Better the devil you know

Stop signs

You are loved, fullstop
You are beauti-full stop

You know yourself best, fullstop

You already have everything to be full
Just stop.

To Me, Love Me

You are amazing.
Never Settle.
Be Brave, you have everything you need and always
will.
Trust your creativity, it was God-given.
I love you and everything will be ok.
I will always be here.

Bonding

Help them help you.
Show them the way, to help you.

On Your Side

Tell the full story.
Your context helps me know you.
Knowing invites compassion.

Waiting

Always remember my little one, it is better to wait for what you want most, than settle for what you have now.

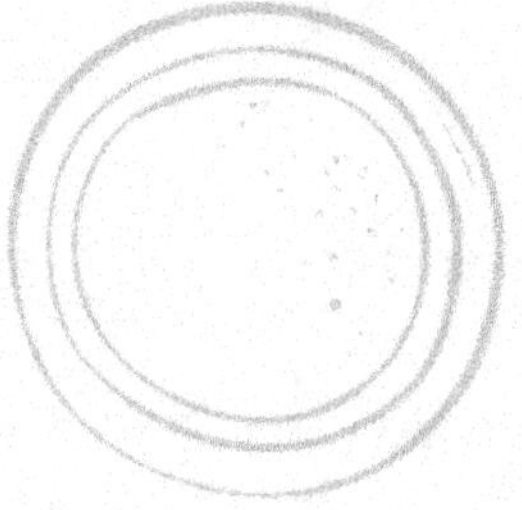

Temptation

I have a never-ending battle between who I am in
this moment, and who I can be at my best.

Figs

Why must we fight,
Hurt,
Break-
Damage each other?
I loved you
And you sliced me open
A hot knife through butter
You slid in
And carved me up
Ready for serving

You ate me for breakfast, lunch
and dinner
Consumed any fruit I produced
Until I was stripped bare
Branches empty

You cursed me
Because I was barren
But before you stole my water and light

I withered
Under 'you may never-'
You rose again

Mathew 21. 18

Cursing of the fig tree
'may you never bear fruit again'

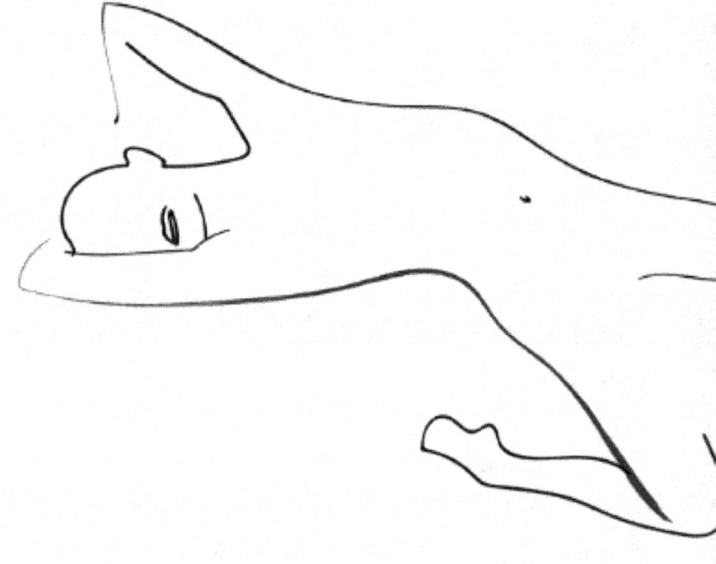

Boundaries

Draw the line
In white chalk
For all to see

The visualise
Manifest steel.

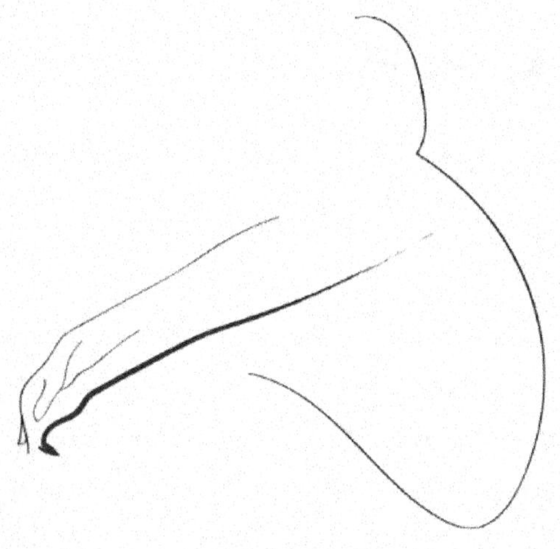

Snake in the Bed

You slithered
In to the withered
Carcass

Of what was

You shed your skin
As you felt
What would serve you best

I had recognised your print
Categorised
Labelled you dangerous.

You acknowledged:
Became something new
Reborn
You invaded the garden
Again, disguised.

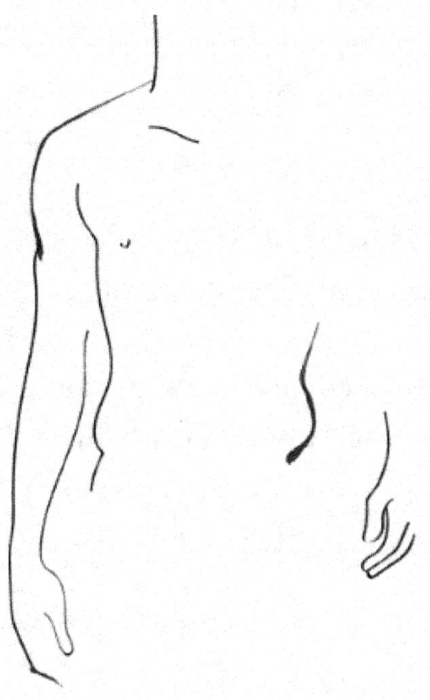

Debt

You do not owe them
Your face, smiles, body
Your time
Your words
Your encouragement
Your patience, kindness, tutorage

For them to become a better person
Needs only their time, effort, will.

Venom.

Do not spend your time with venomous people.

They will drip feed poison
Directly into your bloodstream.

Siren

I Kill myself
Softly
With the song
Of your name

Juliet

The sound
I love you
On your lips
Is a kiss of death

I lean in
Like Juliet
Eager to love
What will be my death

Mercy

Your mercy coats my tongue
Sometimes its sweetness is hard to swallow

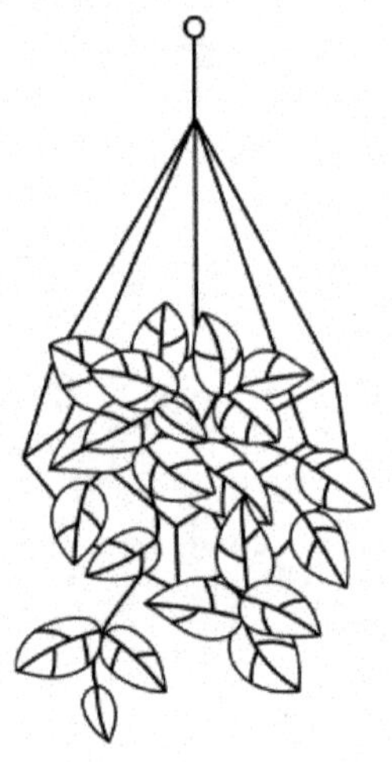

Soul Sisters

After breaking
I rebuild
Through friends and books

Friends in books
Their familiar smiles
Bouncing off the pages
Hello Jo and Laurie,
Jane and Elizabeth
How are your sisters?

Welcome to my table with the Brigerton clan
The Bennets, the Marches.
Come run in a field with me Anne
Show me the lake of shining waters

Belle, invite me to your library
Teach me how to look
Past the Beast of pain
And learn to love what
I have become.

Most importantly
Be careful what you think,
Because thoughts control your life.

Most importantly
Guard your heart.
For everything you do
Everything you say
All you are,
Comes from it.

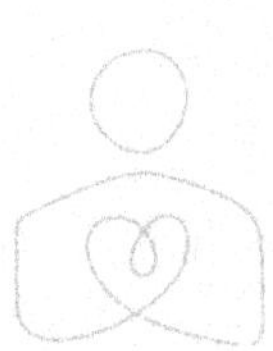

Ministry

I know what I birthed
I see you
And I called you by name
Out of my body and the spirit
Out of my heart and tears
I named you
And called you beautiful
It was good.

The End, or Another Beginning...